Leader's Guide for

WHAT _ _ _ WHEN GOD ANSWERS PRAYER

Evelyn Christenson

Leader's Guide prepared by
DALE AND SANDY LARSEN

Eight Reproducible Response Sheets are included in a removable center section.

A DIVISION OF SCRIPTURE PRESS PUBLICATIONS INC.
USA CANADA ENGLAND

Unless otherwise noted, Scripture quotations are taken from the *Holy Bible, New International Version*®. Copyright © 1973, 1978, 1984 by International Bible Society. Used by permission of Zondervan Publishing House. All rights reserved. Other quotations are from the *Revised Standard Version of the Bible*, (RSV) © 1946, 1952, 1971, 1973; *The New Testament in Modern English* (PH), Revised Edition, © J. B. Phillips, 1958, 1960, 1972, permission of Macmillan Publishing Co. and Collins Publishers; *Good News Bible (Today's English Version)*, (TEV) © American Bible Society 1966, 1971, 1976.

1 2 3 4 5 6 7 8 9 10   Printing/Year 98 97 96 95 94

ISBN: 1-56476-251-3
© 1994 by Victor Books/SP Publications, Inc. All rights reserved.
Printed in the United States of America.

VICTOR BOOKS
A division of SP Publications, Inc.
1825 College Avenue, Wheaton, Illinois 60187

THE PLACE TO BEGIN

Before you start flipping through this Leader's Guide, stop for a couple of minutes and read pages 4–7. These pages will:
- Tell you what you'll need to know to prepare each lesson.
- Introduce different methods of leading group interaction.
- Help you evaluate how you're doing as a group leader.

KNOW YOUR GROUP

Picture the individuals who make up your group. What do you know about them? What do you need to know to lead them effectively? Here are a few suggestions:
- Develop warm relationships—get to know group members by name. Find ways to help members get to know each other as well.
- Find out what your group members already know and what they would like to know.
- Be a good listener.
- Promote an attitude of acceptance and respect among group members.

GET READY TO LEAD

If you are a little unsure of yourself because you're leading a group of adults for the first time, then follow the LESSON PLAN outlines for each session.

Using the guided discovery learning approach, each chapter will contain at least three sections:

- *Launching the Lesson*—activities that begin focusing on group members' needs.
- *Discovering God's Principles*—creative ways to communicate Bible truth.
- *Applying the Truth*—application activities that relate Bible truth to everyday life.

Some sessions may contain additional, optional sections such as:
- *Building the Body*—icebreakers and activities to help group members build relationships.
- *Prayer Time*—suggestions for praying together as a group.

REMEMBER THE BASICS

Read the entire text and this Leader's Guide. Underline important passages in the text and make notes as ideas come to you. Note any activities in the guide that take advance planning or preparation.
Follow these steps in planning each session:
- Make a brief outline of your lesson plan.
- Formulate and *write down* all the discussion questions you intend to use.
- Note all activities and interaction methods you plan to implement.
- Gather all the materials you will need for the session.

Each session should focus on at least one, and often several, Bible truths that can be applied directly to the lives of your group members. Encourage group members to bring their Bibles to each session and use them. It's also a good idea to have several modern-speech translations on hand for the purpose of comparison.

USE A VARIETY OF INTERACTION METHODS

Response Sheets

Several Response Sheets are provided for you in the removable center section of this guide. Response Sheets are designed to extend the lesson's impact.

The Response Sheets in this guide will help you enliven your sessions and encourage group involvement. They are numbered consecutively (Response Sheet 1—Response Sheet 8) and show with what sessions they should be used. The guide gives specific directions for when and how to use each Response Sheet in the lesson material.

Brainstorming

Announce the question or topic to be "stormed." Group members may make as many spontaneous suggestions as possible, not waiting to be called on. Don't allow anyone to criticize the suggestions. List suggestions on a chalkboard or poster board; when all are in, have the class evaluate the ideas. This method loosens up the group, involves nonparticipants, and produces new insights.

Group Bible Study

Each person should have her or his Bible open. Ask questions that will help the group learn what the passage you are studying says. Encourage sharing of insights as the group discusses the interpretations of the passage and its application to current needs. Always summarize findings. This method makes group members think; it shows them how to study the Bible on their own and it increases participation and involvement.

Discovery Groups
Divide the group into small groups of three to six persons. Appoint a leader for each group or let groups select their own leaders. Assign a topic to each group. Several—or all—groups may discuss the same topic if necessary. Allow 5–8 minutes for discussion in the groups, then reconvene and get reports from group leaders. Jot findings on a chalkboard or poster board for discussion. Since many persons are freer to express themselves in small groups, this method provides maximum participation opportunity.

Role Play
Two or more group members, without advance notice or written scripts, act out a situation or relationship. Give them directions as to the kind of people they are to represent and the situation in which they find themselves. They speak extemporaneously. This method helps people "feel" situations, gives them opportunity to try different solutions, and creates interest in the lesson.

Skit
Have members read the parts of a brief script that highlights a point, provokes discussion, or presents information. Skits provide sessions with stimulating variety.

Diads
Like *Discovery Groups*, except that there are only two people, sitting next to each other, in each "group." (If a person is left out in the pairing off, assign him to one of the twosomes.) This method makes it easy for shy persons to participate.

Discussion
In discussion, members interact not only with the group leader but with one another. Usually discussion is started by the group leader's asking a question to which there is more than a single acceptable answer. A member will respond to a question, someone else may disagree with him, and a third person may have additional comments. The leader is responsible for starting the discussion, keeping it "on track" by asking leading questions as necessary, and summarizing it after contributions cease. If a discussion gets out of hand and rambles, much of its value is lost.

Here are a few guidelines for leading discussion:
- Maintain a relaxed, informal atmosphere.

- Don't call on people by name to take part unless you are sure they are willing to do so.
- Give a person lots of time to answer a question. If necessary, restate the question casually and informally.
- Acknowledge any contribution, regardless of its merit.
- Don't correct or embarrass a person who gives a wrong answer. Thank him or her; then ask, "What do the rest of you think?"
- If someone monopolizes the discussion, say, "On the next question, let's hear from someone who hasn't spoken yet."
- If someone goes off on a tangent, wait for him or her to draw a breath, then say, "Thanks for those interesting comments. Now let's get back to . . ." and mention the subject under consideration, or ask or restate a question that will bring the discussion back on target.
- If someone asks a question, allow others in the group to give their answers before you give yours.

EVALUATE YOUR EFFECTIVENESS

After each session, ask yourself the following questions:

_____ How well did each group member understand the lesson goals?

_____ How many group members actually took part in the lesson?

_____ Could I use other interaction methods to increase group member interest and participation?

_____ Did I nurture personal relationships with my group members?

_____ How well did I prepare the lesson?

_____ How did group members react to me as a group leader?

_____ What do I need to do to become a better group leader?

Session One

WHEN GOD ANSWERS...
"HERE IS MY PERSPECTIVE"

TEXT, CHAPTER 1

Session Topic
When God answers a prayer, He expects us to be prepared to act or to be acted on by His answer.

Session Goals
1. To identify times we "close the book" on God's answers and fail to ask what He intends to accomplish next.
2. To explore God's perspective on a prayer by Jeremiah, seeing how God's answer fit into His sovereign purpose.
3. To commit ourselves to looking for God's continuing involvement after each answered prayer.

Materials Needed
√ Bible
√ Copies of *What Happens When God Answers Prayer* for the group
√ A copy of Response Sheet 1 for each person
√ Pencils
√ Chalkboard, chalk

Special Preparation
1. Recall times that God answered your prayers and you then "closed the book" on the incident. Consider whether events that followed were evidence of God's continuing involvement.
2. To get the context of the lesson Scripture, read Jeremiah 32–33. In 587 B.C., because of Judah's idolatry, God allowed Jerusalem to be besieged by the Babylonians under Nebuchadnezzar. Jeremiah was arrested for prophesying that Jerusalem would fall. In the midst of impending disaster, God directed

Jeremiah to purchase a field. Jeremiah obeyed, but not understanding God's purpose in this, he prayed (32:17-25). God answered with a vision not only of Jerusalem's restoration but of the coming of Christ. God had a plan beyond the immediate circumstances. In the same way, He has a plan beyond our own immediate prayers.

LESSON PLAN

Building the Body *(10 minutes)*

Ask group members to share, from their own experiences, brief examples of answered prayer. Explain that you must emphasize "brief" so as many people as possible can speak up. Do not insist that every person say something, because some members may be new to prayer or may not be able to identify a specific answer.

Launching the Lesson *(10 minutes)*

Say: **We've come together to talk about "What happens when God answers." Notice we aren't saying "What happens *if* God answers," but "when." We assume God answers prayer, and we have just been encouraged by each other's stories. Now, when you received those answers to prayer, did you feel the case was closed? Or did you look for what God might want you to do next?** Let members respond.

Distribute copies of Response Sheet 1. After giving members a moment to read, ask: **Would you say that your prayer lives with the Lord are more like "They lived happily ever after" or "To be continued"? And why?** Let group members give responses.

Discovering God's Principles *(25 minutes)*

Ask members to turn to Jeremiah 32:17-25. Explain the background of this prayer: **It was the year 587 B.C., and Jerusalem was under siege by the army of the Babylonian King Nebuchadnezzar. Jeremiah had prophesied that the Babylonians would conquer the city because the Jews had turned to idolatry. That prophecy was not popular. King Zedekiah had Jeremiah arrested and confined to the courtyard of the royal guard. Then God instructed Jeremiah to buy a field outside Jerusalem. Via messenger, Jeremiah obeyed, but then he prayed this prayer.**

Read Jeremiah 32:17-25. Then use the questions below.

- How were the present circumstances confusing to Jeremiah? (He couldn't fit together the imminent conquest of the city and God's direction to purchase a field. What use would a field be to Jeremiah if he became a slave of the Babylonians?)
- What emotional conflicts might Jeremiah have been experiencing? (He had spoken the truth and was under arrest for it. Then God seemed to send him contradictory messages. He would have been tempted to doubt that he was understanding God or even that God was being honest with him.)
- What did Jeremiah acknowledge about the Lord's power and purposes? (Find details in the text.)
- How did Jeremiah's prayer demonstrate faith in God?

Say: God's answer to Jeremiah, on two different occasions, runs from 32:26 to 33:26. God said yes, Nebuchadnezzar would conquer Jerusalem; He also promised that His people would return to live there in safety. Pick out highlights of God's answer by asking people to read 32:28-29; 32:42-44; 33:10-11.

Say: **The heart of God's answer is 33:1-3.** (Read.)

Say: **We often have a two-part approach to prayer: we pray, God answers. But here there is a third part to prayer. First, what was Jeremiah to do?** (Call to the Lord—pray.) **Second, in response to obedient prayer, what did the Lord promise to do first?** (He would answer Jeremiah's immediate prayer.) **Third, what further promise did God make?** (He would go on to reveal great things which Jeremiah could not otherwise know.)

Say: **When Jeremiah called to the Lord, God answered by explaining that the inhabitants of Jerusalem would need their fields in the future. Then God went on to reveal something else which Jeremiah probably did not fully understand at the time.**

- Read Jeremiah 33:14-16. Ask: **How does this promise go far beyond anything Jeremiah prayed?** (It's a promise of the coming Christ, who would not be born for 600 years.)
- **How did God use Jeremiah's prayer as an open door to reveal more about His plans?** (God could have stopped His answer with the restoration of Jerusalem after 70 years, but He went on to reveal the coming of the One who would bring ultimate peace and righteousness to God's people.)

Applying the Truth *(10 minutes)*

The promise of 33:3 was made to the Prophet Jeremiah, but millions of Christians have found it true in their own lives. God not only answers their immediate prayers, He goes on to show them how His answer opens a door to His greater purposes.

Let's brainstorm together a minute. What might be some of God's greater purposes for our lives and the lives of people we care about? As group members give ideas, write them on the chalkboard. If members falter because they try to be too specific, ask them to think of God's will for people in general. Possible answers: salvation of lost, living in holiness, strong and loving families, reconciliation, moral purity, harmony among Christians.

We began by considering God's answers to our prayers. Now we need to consider our response to God's answers. Christenson says, ". . . our response will determine the next state of our spiritual condition, attitude, relationship with God, or arena of activity. Every prayer request, no matter how large or small, always ushers us into our next state. We pray, God answers, and we then decide what to do with His answer."

Discuss:
- How have you responded to God's answer to any of those prayers you mentioned—or thought of—at the beginning of this study? (Wait for thoughtful answers.)
- What do you believe God wants you to do next in response to His answers?
- Regardless of how we have responded to God's past answers, how can we commit ourselves to always looking for what He wants to do next when He answers a prayer?

Prayer Time *(5 minutes)*

Divide your group into groups of three or four. They may pray silently or out loud. Ask them to thank God for answering their prayers, and ask them to commit themselves to looking for what God wants to accomplish next after each answered prayer.

ASSIGNMENT

1. Each time you see a prayer answered this week, look to God for what He might want you to do next.
2. Read chapters 1 and 2 of the text.
3. Consider whether there might be any time when God could not answer a prayer.

Session Two

WHEN GOD ANSWERS... "I AM NOT ABLE"

TEXT, CHAPTER 2

Session Topic
God releases His power through us in response to prayer, but He may choose to limit Himself if we are not faithful in prayer.

Session Goals
1. To discuss how our lack of prayer can limit God's power.
2. To discover how God's power was released through the apostles in response to a specific prayer.
3. To plan faithful praying in areas we have been neglecting.

Materials Needed
√ Bible
√ *What Happens When God Answers Prayer*
√ Four cards, each with one of the following versions of a phrase from Ephesians 3:20
 "immeasurably more than all we ask or imagine" (NIV);
 "far more abundantly than all we ask or think" (RSV);
 "infinitely more than we ever dare to ask or imagine" (PH);
 "so much more than we can ever ask for, or even think of" (TEV).
√ Lists of discussion questions under *Discovering God's Principles* for each group leader
√ Chalkboard, chalk
√ Response Sheet 2 for each person

Special Preparation
1. The Scripture for this lesson records the sort of dramatic event which believers do not normally experience in everyday pray-

11

ing. Try to relate it to experience by recalling times you prayed in the face of seemingly impossible opposition, and the Holy Spirit gave you strength to continue to do what was right.
2. Read Acts 3 and 4 to understand the conflict that led up to the believers' prayer in Acts 4:24-30.
3. Consider areas of your own life where you say you want to see God at work, but for which you are not always faithful to pray.

LESSON PLAN

Launching the Lesson *(10 minutes)*

Ask a provocative question: **Is there anything God can't do?** Divide the group into pairs to briefly discuss the question before you ask for responses. Allow all speculations without arguing for or against them. Don't aim to settle the question, but aim to help group members think about God's power from a variety of angles.

Discovering God's Principles *(30 minutes)*

Say: Like us, the early Christians often prayed in emergency situations. One dramatic example appears in Acts 4. Not long after Pentecost, Peter and John healed a crippled man in the name of Jesus. The event caused such a stir that religious authorities jailed them and ordered them not to speak or teach in Jesus' name—an order the apostles said they couldn't obey. Peter and John won a temporary victory of release, but it was obvious these confrontations were just starting. So the Christians prayed.

Read aloud their prayer and God's response in Acts 4:23-31.

If your group is large, subdivide into small groups and give a list of these questions to each leader.

- After Peter and John reported what had happened, how promptly did the believers pray?
- With what words or phrases did the believers express their confidence in God's power?
- What did they expect God to do?
- After they prayed and the building was shaken, what were the believers empowered to do?
- What do you think were the results of God's power at work in the believers?

After a time, call everyone back to share their findings.

Display Visual Sketch 1 and discuss it.

Introduce Ephesians 3:20 by giving one of the four cards to four group members. Ask each in turn to read the card aloud. After each person reads, ask: **What does that phrase say to you?** Explain that these are various translations of the phrase from Ephesians 3:20. Compare the various phrasings to communicate a sense of the unlimited power of God.

Now look at the phrase in context by asking group members to turn to Ephesians 3:20. If members have various Bible translations, ask them to read the entire verse aloud to each other.

As believers, we have all of God living and working within us, but we know by experience that God's power in us is sometimes stifled and hindered. Evelyn Christenson believes that God sometimes allows Himself to be limited by us—specifically, by our lack of prayer. She writes: "Even though God can do anything He wants, He has chosen to permit us to limit many of His actions by our lack of faithfulness in prayer. Conversely, our sufficient praying will enable Him to give the answers we both desire" (p. 14).

Lead the group to weigh those statements against their own experience by saying: **Evelyn has found that God releases His power through us in response to prayer—and that God allows His power to be blocked by our lack of prayer. How have you found either of those ideas confirmed in your own experience?**

At this point it will be good to counteract an immature view of Christian prayer: that God's power is a convenient force we can call on at any time to get us out of a jam. Point out to your group:

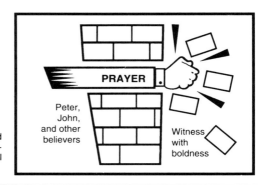

Visual Sketch 1
The prayers of believers knocked down the wall of the authorities' opposition and opened the way to powerful witness in Jerusalem.

God's power is not some sort of magic which we can conjure up by saying the right words or using the right formula. He works within us to glorify Himself and accomplish His purposes, not to grant us our every desire. We can expect to see God's power released through us when our purposes are the same as His.

Applying the Truth *(10 minutes)*

Write the word POWER vertically down the left side of the chalkboard. Say: **Let's think of areas of life beginning with each of these letters where we would like to see God working with power—but which we often neglect to pray about.**

Write answers as group members call them out. For example:

Political leaders, President, People in need, Pastor
Office (people at, conflicts at)
War, Winning people to Christ
Education (schools) in our community
Repentance (national, personal), Relief organizations

Discuss: **How can we plan to pray more faithfully about these things and other areas of life where we want to see God at work?** (Writing down reminders is a simple but effective tool for prayer. We should also ask ourselves how much we really care about those people and issues. Another vital question is whether we want God's will or our own will in those areas.)

Prayer Time *(10 minutes)*

Spend this time praying for the needs you wrote on the chalkboard and for others which you may have been neglecting. If you have enough group members, divide into five small groups and ask each to begin by praying for the things listed under one of the five letters of POWER. Then they can go on to pray for other needs.

ASSIGNMENT

Pass out Response Sheet 2 and make the following assignments:
1. Study Christ's words in John 15:1-8.
2. Make notes on Response Sheet 2 indicating your ideas about some good and bad reasons for praying.
3. Read chapter 3 of the text.

Session Three

WHEN GOD ANSWERS... "YOU PRAYED THE WRONG PRAYER"

TEXT, CHAPTER 3

Session Topic
We must examine the motives for our prayers, because God may deny our prayers when we pray for the wrong reasons.

Session Goals
1. To discover wrong reasons which might motivate "good" prayers.
2. To examine what James wrote and what Jesus said about good and bad motives for prayer.
3. To evaluate the motives behind our own unanswered prayers.

Materials Needed
√ Bibles
√ *What Happens When God Answers Prayer*
√ A copy of Response Sheet 2 for each person (these were handed out to members at the end of Session 2); extras for newcomers
√ Pencils
√ (Optional) Two house plants: one that is full and healthy because it has been pinched back as it grew, and one that has been allowed to get spindly and weak

Special Preparation
1. The word translated "prunes" in John 15:2 also means "cleanses." It is the Greek *kathairo,* from which we get *catharsis.* The Father's pruning is not simply a removal of externals but an internal cleansing of our motives.
2. "The purposes of pruning are various: to keep plants healthy, to restrict or to promote growth, to encourage bloom, or to

15

repair damage. . . . Fruit growers prune to get bigger, better fruit and to prolong the life of their trees. . . . In every case, the purpose of pruning is to get more out of a plant" (John Philip Baumgardt, *How to Prune Almost Everything*, New York: Wm. Morrow & Co., 1968, p. 7).
3. Reflect on how the Lord has "pruned" your life by trimming away wrong attitudes and motives. Consider how those wrong attitudes and motives might have affected your prayers.

LESSON PLAN

Building the Body (Optional) *(5 minutes)*

Show your group the two house plants and ask what they think caused the difference between them. Explain that the healthy plant has been pruned back—that is, unnecessary shoots were cut off. The weaker plant was left to grow as it pleased with no trimming back.

Ask: **If the plant that was pruned back had feelings, how do you think it felt about those scissors cutting off its nice-looking shoots?** (To the plant, the pruning would have felt like severe injury, even a threat to its life. It would have thought those shoots were valuable and necessary.)

Sometimes our prayers reach out to God the way the branches of the spindly plant reach out—but they don't bear fruit because our reasons are not right.

Launching the Lesson *(10 minutes)*

Ask your group: **Why should we pray?** Try to lead members to think of our personal motives and reasons for praying, beyond "Because God wants us to"—though that is certainly true. Then ask: **Why should we not pray? Or to rephrase it, what are some motives which could negate our prayers?**

Evelyn Christenson says, "While most of us are careful basically to pray for things we believe are good, and which God wants to grant us, we usually are completely unaware of the wrong motives that can be inspiring those prayers. And praying with wrong motives for things to which God usually answers yes spells failure in prayer."

Discovering God's Principles *(30 minutes)*

Say: Nobody has perfect reasons for praying every prayer. On the other hand we want our hearts to be as pure as possible when we talk with God. We need to make a practice of examining our motives for prayer. We don't want God to have to say no when He longs to say yes. We're going to look at two Scriptures which give negative and positive aspects of motivations for prayer.

Ask a group member to read James 4:1-3.
Discuss:
- This passage gives a pretty blunt reason for unanswered prayer. What is it?
- What would be an example of a good prayer prayed for the wrong reason? (Give group members time to offer several examples. This is not a cheerful passage. During the discussion, try to be aware if some group members with tender consciences might come under a false sense of condemnation. The Scripture passage from John should help offset James' bluntness.)

Read Evelyn Christenson's list of some common wrong motives that can creep into our praying: **praise, fame, love of power, love of display, love of preeminence, status over others, ease, comfort, personal satisfaction, self-pleasing, self-vindication, gratification of sinful desires, even revenge.**
- In this passage from James, quarreling and wrong motives for prayer are bound up with each other. How do the motives I just read promote quarreling among Christians? (You will probably need to refer the group to the list on page 28 of *What Happens When God Answers Prayer*. All those qualities lead to strife among Christians because they are all some form of self-promotion at the cost of others. They promote jealousy and competition among believers.)
- Why is it so hard for us to detect these motives in ourselves? (Perhaps we don't think that a praying Christian could possibly approach God with such motives. Also the *results* of our prayers may be in line with God's will, even though our motives are opposed. For example, we may pray for success for our church's evangelistic ministry—which God also wants—but we want success so our church will look good or will grow numerically.)

Say: **Notice that James doesn't tell us to stop praying. He** encourages us to ask God for what we want—but with the right motivations. This passage feels negative, but it is God's Word and it is honest with us.

Not long before He was crucified, Jesus talked about motives for prayer. Ask another group member to read John 15:1-8. Discuss:

- **Before Jesus spoke of asking God for anything, He described our relationship with Him. How?** (Discuss how strongly attached a branch must be to the central vine in order to live at all, let alone bear any fruit.)
- **What unpleasantness do the branches have to undergo in order to be more fruitful?** (Being pruned back by the gardener, the Father. Point out that the Greek word translated "prunes" also means "cleanses," from the same root as our English word *catharsis*.)
- **After describing our relationship with Him, how does Jesus mention prayer?** (As a promise with a condition, v. 7.)
- **What condition does He put on the promise of answered prayer?** (Answered prayer comes from a continuing close relationship between Christ and us.)
- **What is a possible relationship between unanswered prayer and our motivations?** (Direct the group to get out their copies of Response Sheet 2, on which they should have made some notations. Divide into small groups and have members compare and discuss their answers. Allow time for members to write down new ideas and for members who failed to do the assignment to come up with some responses.)

Call members back into one group and ask for volunteers to give responses of both "fruitful" and "pruned" reasons for praying.

Applying the Truth *(10 minutes)*

Direct members to look again at their Response Sheets. Ask: **In your own prayer life, are there motives that should be pruned but are still trying to hang on?** Have members draw additional "pruned" branches lying shriveled beside the vine—attitudes from which they want God to cleanse them. Allow silent time for this introspective exercise. Then ask for anyone to volunteer to share an answer or two, so members can pray for one other's cleansing. It will be helpful to other members if you are honest and share a motivation you would like the Lord to "prune."

Say: Not every unanswered prayer is the result of wrong motives. As Evelyn Christenson writes, our timing is not always God's timing. Perhaps we are not ready, or others are not ready, or the answer to that prayer is for someone else and not for us. Among the many reasons for unanswered prayer, today we are concentrating on wrong motives as a possible explanation. When our prayers are not answered, it's never a bad idea to examine our reasons for praying.

Prayer Time *(10 minutes)*

Focus today's prayer time on the cleansing of your hearts from wrong motives. Even as you pray for requests from other members, add prayers that your motives for praying will be right. Surrender the objects of prayer to God and tell Him you want His will to be done.

ASSIGNMENT

Ask that during the week your group members:
1. Take note of how God might be pruning away wrong motives for their prayers, in answer to today's praying.
2. Read chapter 4 of the text.
3. Recall special Scripture God has given them just when needed.

Session Four

WHEN GOD ANSWERS... "I PRERECORDED THAT ANSWER"

TEXT, CHAPTER 4

Session Topic
God frequently answers our prayers by guiding us to a Scripture that contains the answer.

Session Goals
1. To consider various "tones of voice" God might use in speaking through Scripture.
2. To describe some ways God uses Scripture to answer our prayers.
3. To recommit ourselves to respond to the Author as we read His Word.

Materials Needed
√ Bible
√ *What Happens When God Answers Prayer*
√ 3 x 5 cards on which you have written various moods such as: angry, uncertain, pleading, joyful, impatient, fearful, authoritative, disbelieving, and so forth.
√ Chalkboard, chalk
√ A list of the questions in *Discovering God's Principles* for each leader

Special Preparation
1. Recall times God used a specific Scripture to answer a need you were praying about. Try to remember how you were led to each passage.
2. If you choose to use a different sentence than the one suggested in *Launching the Lesson,* come up with an alternative.

LESSON PLAN

Launching the Lesson *(5 minutes)*

Distribute the 3 x 5 cards to individuals, asking them not to show the cards to anyone else. Write this sentence on the chalkboard: "I think there are going to be a lot of changes at work in the near future." Call on the people with the cards to read the sentence using the tone of voice indicated on the card. After each person reads, ask the group to guess the mood which is on the card.

Thank your readers. Say: **Evelyn Christenson points out that many times we pray for answers, and God replies, "I already told you that. I have prerecorded that answer in the Bible."** Evelyn says that, when God answers our prayers through His Word, He does not chant in a monotone. He speaks to us in various "tones of voice," something like the people who just read this sentence to us.

Discovering God's Principles *(35 minutes)*

Explain: **As we read God's "prerecorded answers" to our prayers, sometimes His voice is comforting. Sometimes He rebukes us gently or firmly. Sometimes He pleads with us, or reasons with us, or makes a bold declaration. His Word speaks to us in different ways at different times, depending on our needs.**

Read aloud 2 Timothy 3:14-17. Point out that Paul was reminding his younger friend Timothy of Timothy's background in the Scriptures and his responsibility to continue in them, but in verses 16-17 Paul also spoke about how God speaks to us through Scripture.

Using the questions below, discuss how God speaks to us through His Word as we pray. It is easy for a group to begin to discuss what it means for Scripture to be "inspired" or "God-breathed" in verse 16, but keep this discussion centered on how God uses Scripture in our lives. If you wish, divide into subgroups and give each group leader a list of the discussion questions.

- If we are going to pray for God to teach us through His Word, what attitudes of heart and mind do we need?
- How can we pray about our natural defensiveness when God rebukes us through His Word?
- Why would prayerfully studying the life of Christ lead naturally to our being corrected by God?

- If we are praying that God will help us live rightly, how can Scripture train us to live that way?
- Why would neglecting the Bible leave us unequipped for the good work God wants us to do? (Sample answers: We would be left guessing about God's will. We might do the right things but with un-Christlike attitudes. We wouldn't know God's priorities. We would not understand how different people have different gifts for different ministries and might try to do everything ourselves or do things we're not fit for.)

If you have divided into subgroups, call everyone back into one large group and discuss some of their responses.

Say: Evelyn Christenson relates four ways that she believes God uses to speak to her through His Word in answer to her prayers. Sometimes He shows her the answer in the portion of Scripture she is reading devotionally. At other times God brings to mind a thought or a clue that tells her where in the Bible she should look for the answer. Occasionally He reminds her of a book of the Bible, a chapter, even a place on a page. And sometimes she randomly turns to a page and sees the answer staring right at her.

Help the group see that for the Lord to lead us through His Word in such specific ways, we must be closely involved with Him. We won't have such experiences of guidance if we look on the Bible as just a rule book or storybook written long ago by a stranger.

Have someone read John 14:25-27. Remind your group that Jesus was about to die and leave His disciples seemingly alone. He was reassuring them that through His Spirit, He would continue to teach them and bring them peace. Explain that as the Holy Spirit brought about the remembrance of Jesus' words, His followers passed them on verbally and later wrote them down. Through the centuries, as people have read this book, the Holy Spirit has continued to bring it to life and apply it to each heart.

Discuss:
- What kind of relationship is portrayed between Jesus' followers and the Holy Spirit?
- The Bible is the only book whose Author is always present when it is read. What difference would it make in our Bible reading and our prayers if we stayed aware that the Author is always present as we are reading? (Our Bible reading would be more intimately combined with prayer,

because we would frequently ask Him for further enlightenment on something we've read or how we should apply it to ourselves. We would also treat His written Word with more respect because of our respect for Him.)

Summarize this chapter's teaching about God's prerecorded answers to prayer by saying: **Often God has prerecorded His answer to our prayer, but as Evelyn Christenson says, three steps are necessary to use God's prerecorded answer effectively: (1) accept it, (2) respond to its Author, and (3) live it. We often want to bypass number 2, either refusing to obey or trying hard to obey in our own strength. God, the Author of the answers to our prayers, wants to be involved in our lives to give us the wisdom, grace, strength, power, and, most important, the desire to apply the answers.**

Applying the Truth *(10 minutes)*

Pose these questions for each group member to consider silently: **When you read God's Word, do you tend to skip over the step of responding to the Author? Or do you give the Holy Spirit a chance to interact with you and lead you into His truth?**

Discuss briefly:
- **How can we give God more opportunity to speak to us through His Word when we pray?** (Allow more time and more quietness when we are reading; don't just read the Bible "on the run." Pray with our Bibles open. Pause during our praying and listen to what God might be bringing to mind—a verse, a reference, a word, an idea, a person in the Bible.)

Prayer Time *(10 minutes)*

Divide the group (including yourself) into pairs or threes to pray for each other. Encourage everyone to pray for more openness to the Lord's voice speaking through His Word. Pray for more faithfulness in reading and studying the Bible.

ASSIGNMENT

1. Ask group members to read chapter 5 of the text.
2. Leave the group with this question to consider: *What is the difference between personality quirks and sins?*

Session Five

WHEN GOD ANSWERS... "YOU HAVE NOT FULFILLED MY REQUIREMENTS"

TEXT, CHAPTER 5

Session Topic
God places some conditions on answering our prayers. He answers only when we are willing to be and do what He requires.

Session Goals
1. To introduce the idea of why we set conditions for the granting of some requests.
2. To make clear that sin blocks God from answering prayer.
3. To admit sins that are keeping God from answering our prayers.

Materials Needed
√ Bible
√ *What Happens When God Answers Prayer*
√ Coupons which have requirements or conditions on them, such as "with separate $10 purchase" or an expiration date (for *Building the Body*)
√ "Help Wanted" ads from a newspaper (for *Launching the Lesson*)
√ Copies of Response Sheet 3
√ Pencils

Special Preparation
1. Consider areas of your life—especially in ministry—where you feel powerless. Ask the Lord to reveal any hidden sin which might be hindering His power from working through you.
2. Read 2 Samuel 11 and 12, the background of Psalm 51.
3. Ask a good reader to be prepared to read Psalm 51 aloud.

LESSON PLAN

Building the Body (5 minutes)

Get group members thinking about "requirements" for getting something desirable. Say that today you are giving away coupons. Distribute coupons and ask people to find any requirements stated on the coupon. A requirement might be "good with $10 purchase," an expiration date, "good 4–9 P.M. only," "only at stores with deli," or any other restriction. Let members keep the coupons.

Launching the Lesson (10 minutes)

Distribute "Help Wanted" ads. Say: **These ads are a little like the coupons. They include strict requirements, this time for something more serious than laundry soap or a hamburger. These are requirements for getting a job.** Ask members to pick out job requirements from the ads, such as experience, education, or skills.

Help members think about the purpose of setting requirements. Ask: **What would happen if employers set no conditions for workers doing particular jobs?** (Workers would not be matched with work they can do well. People would be trying to do things for which they are incompetent, causing lots of confusion and problems, possibly even danger. The employer and employee would both be disgraced.)

Introduce the idea that God sets conditions on answered prayer by saying: **If employers set conditions for workers, God certainly has the right to set conditions for answering our prayers. But why would God set conditions? Why not just answer all prayers regardless of who asks or why?** (Let group members discuss this a few minutes.) **To understand why God sets conditions on answered prayer, we should look at what His conditions are.**

Discovering God's Principles (30 minutes)

Remind your group that a few weeks ago you looked at John 15:7: "If you remain in Me and My words remain in you, ask whatever you wish, and it will be given you." Point out that a little later Jesus also said, "I chose you and appointed you to go and bear fruit—fruit that will last. Then the Father will give you whatever you ask in My name" (John 15:16).

■ Jesus promises to give us anything we ask for—if. What

25

conditions does Jesus set on answered prayer? (Remaining in Him, His words remaining in us, bearing lasting fruit, asking in His name.)
- Those conditions are not so much conditions like rules on a coupon as a description of a trusting walk with Christ. What words would you use to describe the relationship between us and Christ which is the condition of answered prayer? (During the discussion, remind your group of the vine and branches which you used on Response Sheet 2. This is a picture of a close and continuing relationship between us, the pray-ers, and Christ, the prayer-answerer.)
- What do you think it means to ask for something "in His name"? (Asking for something Jesus would ask the Father for; asking for something Jesus could "sign His name" to. When we're close to Him, we naturally ask for things in His will rather than outside it.)
- How would hidden sin—that is, unconfessed sin—affect the close relationship between us and Christ?

Introduce the background of Psalm 51 by saying: **At one point, King David thought he could hide sin with no disruption in his relationship with God. David committed adultery with Bathsheba, and when he found out she was pregnant, he had her husband killed in battle and married her. He thought he had gotten away with all this through his own cleverness.**

Discuss: **The Bible does not tell us specifically, but how do you think David's prayers were affected when he put himself in such a hypocritical relationship with God?**

Introduce Psalm 51, David's psalm of confession: **God's remedy for this terrible situation was not cleverness—it was confrontation, confession, and forgiveness. God still loved David, so much that He sent Nathan the prophet to confront him. When David confessed, he found his broken relationship with the Lord wonderfully restored. He wrote about it in Psalm 51.**

Tell group members to turn in their Bibles to Psalm 51. Have your reader (whom you asked earlier) read the psalm aloud.

Lead the group to consider the question you assigned them last week. Say: **It takes humility to confess, but it also takes courage. David was courageous enough to call sin by its true name: sin. Some people would have called his actions with Bathsheba a weakness or a quirk of personality. What do you think is the difference?** (David deliberately planned and carried out actions which he knew were morally wrong. He took full responsibility.

That's very different from trying to call it a mistake, a weakness, or an eccentricity.)

Read verse 13, where David wrote *"Then I will teach transgressors Your ways, and sinners will turn back to You."* Note that David meant "after I have confessed and You have forgiven my sin." Point out that the power of God was not going to flow through David to minister to others until David himself was clean of hidden sin.

Compare David's experience with the text by saying: **Evelyn Christenson has found the same conditions on power in her prayer ministry. People sometimes think she is a Superwoman who never struggles with sin. But she says that the more she works to be holy, the more God reveals her sin—such as pride, wrong attitudes, wrong priorities, or disobedience. Evelyn discovered that if she is concealing any sin, her ministry will be only in her own strength and there will be no moving of God's Spirit in her prayer seminars. She writes: "The greatest deterrent to my sinning or allowing unconfessed sin in my life is knowing that there will be no power in my ministry. This is my responsibility"** (p. 67).

Applying the Truth (10 minutes)

Distribute Response Sheet 3. Explain: **It's never pleasant to search our hearts for unconfessed sin, but David found that the pain was worth it because it restored his relationship with God. If there is any unconfessed sin that is hindering God from answering our prayers, David's psalm of confession can help us see it and confess it.** Have group members complete Response Sheet 3 individually with their Bibles open to Psalm 51.

Prayer Time (5 minutes)

Invite the group to pray silently about what they have just written on their Response Sheets. As they pray, they may want to write notes of confession and thanks to the Lord on the sheet.

Close your time of silent personal prayer by praying aloud a prayer of thanksgiving for God's forgiveness.

ASSIGNMENT

Ask group members to read chapter 6 of the text.

Session Six

WHEN GOD ANSWERS... "REPENT"

TEXT, CHAPTER 6

Session Topic
True repentance means turning away from sin and turning to God.

Session Goals
1. To illustrate changing our minds, with resulting actions.
2. To develop the idea that biblical repentance is a good process, though sorrowful.
3. To pray for true repentance and the fruit repentance brings.

Materials Needed
√ Bible
√ *What Happens When God Answers Prayer*
√ Two sealed envelopes: one with blank paper folded around a dollar bill, the other with only blank paper (for *Building the Body*)
√ Copies of Response Sheet 4
√ Pencils
√ (Optional) For *Launching the Lesson,* a flattering photograph or painting of yourself, and a mirror

Special Preparation
1. Most of us can remember when we repented of our sin and accepted Christ. Think of times since then when the Lord has brought you to repentance—the kind of repentance Evelyn Christenson calls "the Christian reestablishing a God-pleasing lifestyle."
2. Thank God for the sorrow of seeing your sin as He sees it, because that vision leads you to repent and forsake those sins and brings you closer to Him.

attern of prayer with the Lord?

yer.
r class purposes only.

The Vine—Christ (John 15:1-8

Label the "fruitful" branches and the "pruné

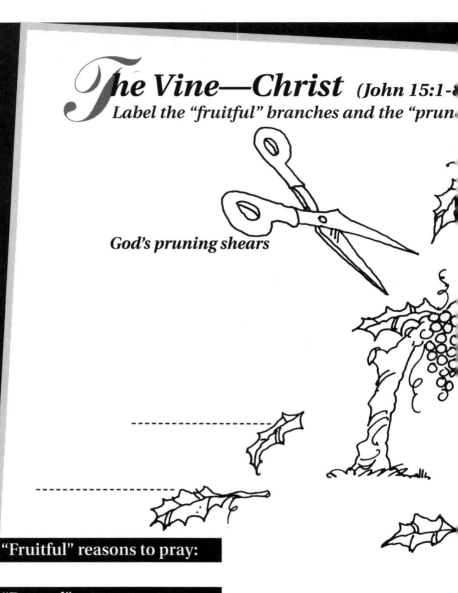

God's pruning shears

"Fruitful" reasons to pray:

"Pruned" reasons to pray:

so that you are proved right when you speak
and justified when you judge.

Create in me a pure heart, O God,
and renew a steadfast spirit within me.
Do not cast me from your presence
or take your Holy Spirit from me.
Restore to me the joy of your salvation
and grant me a willing spirit, to sustain me.

Then I will teach transgressors your ways,
and sinners will turn back to you.

The 180° Corinthian Turn

→ dissensions   → rebelling against God's authority

← readiness to see justice done   ← concern   ← longing   ← alarm

- Why does repentance cause sorrow?
- What is the difference between godly sorrow and worldly
- How had the Corinthians demonstrated that they had ac
- What fruit was their repentance producing?
- If you were a member of the Corinthian church, what en
- How is Paul a good example for anyone who has had to c

self

What we can do	How God provided all this

How I have felt when someone has sinned against me:

_____

_____

_____

What I have lost:

_____

_____

_____

What I wish the person who sinned against me would do:

_____

_____

_____

What I learn from:

1 Thessalonians 5:24

Isaiah 55:10-13

Matthew 25:14-21

Ephesians 3:14-21

"But I can — and will"

My Prayer Attitudes

When I pray, it is usually with an attitude of _____.

Here are the attitudes I usually have when making requests to God concerning:

Family members: _____ (name)

_____ (name)

Health: _____

Work: _____

Church: _____

Response Sheet 8 Use with session 12 of *What Happens When God Answers*
© 1994 by SP Publications, Inc. Permission granted to purchaser to reproduce this Response Sheet

Physical/material needs:

_____
(other)

_____
(a deep, ongoing need)

My Request

ayer.
class purposes only.

"Lord, I can't"

Ways the Lord me to obey Hi

Reasons I feel inadequate:

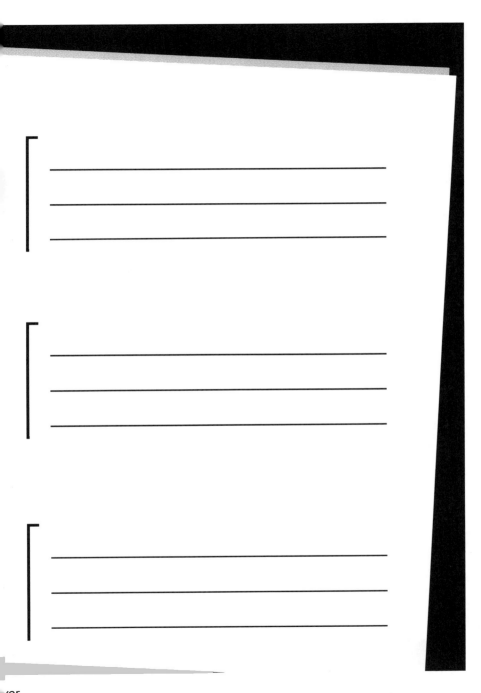

God Reconciles Us to Him

Romans 5:1-11	What we have
1–5	
6–8	
9–11	

Response Sheet 5 Use with session 7 of *What Happens When God Answers P*
© 1994 by SP Publications, Inc. Permission granted to purchaser to reproduce this Response Sheet

(2 Corinthians 7:8-12)

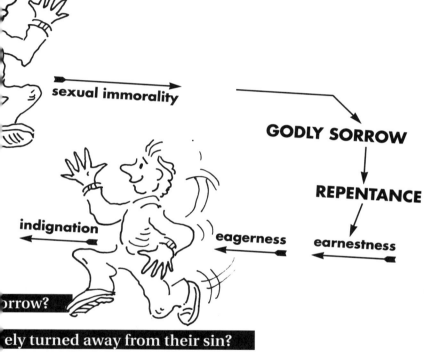

orrow?

ely turned away from their sin?

uragement would you find in Paul's words?

front a sinner?

er.
class purposes only.

Psalm 51 —
David's Prayer...and Mine

Have mercy on me, O God, for _____
according to your unfailing love;
according to your great compassion
blot out my transgressions of _____
Wash away all my iniquity
and cleanse me from my sin of _____

For I know my transgressions,
and my sin is always before me.
Against you, you only, have I sinned

" *branches*

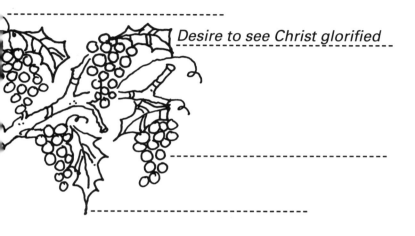

Desire to see Christ glorified

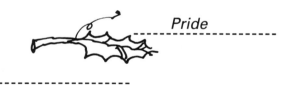

Pride

Which story most resembles the story of you

Why do you respond as you do?

Response Sheet 1 Use with session 1 of *What Happens When God Answers*
© 1994 by SP Publications, Inc. Permission granted to purchaser to reproduce this Response Sheet

3. In the Greek, the word "repent" is *metanoeo,* literally "to perceive afterward," from *meta* (after) and *noeo* (to perceive). It "signifies to change one's mind or purpose, always, in the New Testament, involving a change for the better, an amendment, and always, except in Luke 17:3-4, of repentance from sin" (W.E. Vine, *An Expository Dictionary of New Testament Words* vol. III (London: Oliphants Ltd., 1940), 279–80).

LESSON PLAN

Building the Body *(5 minutes)*

Ask for a volunteer to choose between two sealed envelopes. After the volunteer has taken one, say: **I think it's only fair to tell you that one of these envelopes has money in it; the other doesn't. Do you want to change your mind about which one you take?** Give the volunteer one opportunity to change his or her mind, then have the volunteer open the envelope picked.

Thank your volunteer. Say: **Changing our minds about things always produces results. So does failing to change our minds. Our volunteer, (insert name), was in the dark about which choice to make. But God lets us know His moral law, and if we've made the wrong choices, He clearly tells us to change our minds. That's what the Bible calls repentance.**

Launching the Lesson *(10 minutes)*

Last week we looked at confession of sin as a requirement for answered prayer and for God's power to flow through us. As we could see from David's prayer in Psalm 51, confession is more than a quick "I'm sorry, Lord." Confession should lead to repentance.

Evelyn Christenson points out several things that God does *not* say about repentance. He does not ask, "Would you like to repent?" or say, "It would be nice if you did." When we admit a sin, He does not say, "That's okay, let's just forget it." God sees our sin as it really is, and He calls us to turn away from it.

Use this question to introduce the idea of "seeing ourselves as God sees us" (if you brought the picture and mirror, display them as you ask the question): **Which would you rather face the first thing in the morning: a flattering picture of yourself or a mirror?** (Most people would probably rather face the flattering picture. Others may note that the portrait does not really help you face the world, because it doesn't tell you the truth about the face you should wash or the hair you should comb.)

Make the connection with repentance by saying: **The mirror lets us see ourselves as others see us. Why does seeing ourselves as God sees us lead us to repentance?** (We see our sin in contrast to God's holiness. If we care about Him, we are grieved that we have hurt Him and hurt the people He loves.)

Discovering God's Principles *(25 minutes)*

Evelyn Christenson believes that repentance has three parts: being truly sorrowful for our sin, actively turning away from it, and bringing forth fruit in keeping with repentance. To repent is to stop going one way, turn around, and start going the opposite way. It's a 180-degree turn. In 2 Corinthians we read Paul's approving words for some people who repented in that way.

Distribute Response Sheet 4. Explain the background of the Scripture passage: Paul had begun the church in Corinth, but after leaving, he heard that some had turned away. They were splitting into factions, rebelling against God's authority, and practicing flagrant sexual immorality. Paul wrote them a stern letter and apparently paid them a visit which resulted in a painful confrontation. Now he had heard through Titus that the Corinthians had truly repented. Have someone read 2 Corinthians 7:8-12. Use the Response Sheet to discuss:

- **Why does repentance cause sorrow?** (We see ourselves as we are, stripped of self-justification and deception.)
- **What is the difference between godly sorrow and worldly sorrow?** (Worldly sorrow might be remorse, feeling sorry for ourselves, or regretting the trouble our sin got us into. Godly sorrow is how we feel when we realize how we have hurt God.)
- **How had the Corinthians demonstrated that they had actively turned away from their sin?** (They had godly sorrow and then they set about amending their lives.)
- **What fruit was their repentance producing?** (They had stopped fighting Paul and God, and they were making moral change.)
- **If you were a member of the Corinthian church, what encouragement would you find in Paul's words?** (Paul let them know he knew about the change in their lives and he

commended them. When we're trying to make positive changes, it is always encouraging to know the changes are noticed and approved.)
- **How is Paul a good example for anyone who has had to confront a sinner?** (Paul had been successful, but he didn't gloat or act superior toward the Corinthians. He let them know he was on their side by encouraging and praising their new actions.)

Applying the Truth *(10 minutes)*

Summarize what Evelyn Christenson says about revival and repentance: We would all like those bad sinners "out there" to repent, but Evelyn Christenson says that when God calls for repentance, He begins with His people—us. She tells of calling leaders from across the United States to participate in a prayer conference for national revival. They met, but God surprised them. They spent the first half of the conference repenting for their own sin, before they even started praying for others to repent.
- **How do you respond to the idea that God calls His own people to repent before we can call others to repent?**
- **Evelyn reports that as the conference participants prayed, she was shocked at the seemingly inconsequential and trivial attitudes and actions which God kept bringing up to them as sin. How do you feel about spending so much time and energy in introspection? Does it distract us from the real work of God? Or do you see value in searching out and repenting of the smallest things?** (Help members see that attitudes and habits we call trivial may be very serious to God. For example, we usually excuse gossip and lustful thoughts as minor infractions, but God says they cause great damage in relationships. However, it's also true that too much introspection can be an escape from dealing with the world.)
- **As a group (or as a church), how ready do you think we are to pray for revival in our community or nation?** (If your group is not accustomed to the word "revival," rephrase the question something like: How ready do you think we are to pray for people to repent of their sin and come to Christ? Don't attempt to get a final answer, because this will probably be a touchy question. Some people in your group may think that *others* in the group need to repent, which is exactly the

flaw Evelyn Christenson writes about—thinking somebody else needs to repent before I do!)

Prayer Time *(10 minutes)*

Call members' attention back to Response Sheet 4. Point out again what a good thing "godly sorrow" is and how true repentance produces good fruit. Divide into subgroups or stay in one large group, as you wish. Explain that you will spend this prayer time praying for yourselves, asking the Lord to show each of you where you need to repent. No one has to reveal any sins out loud. It's all right if there is a lot of silence during this prayer time as you let the Lord speak to your hearts.

Close your time of prayer by singing an appropriate hymn or praise song. If people in your group are not singers, prayerfully read the words together.

ASSIGNMENT

1. Encourage members to keep searching their hearts this week and repenting of any sin the Lord shows them.
2. Read Chapter 7 of the text.

Session Seven

WHEN GOD ANSWERS...
"BE RECONCILED TO ME"

TEXT, CHAPTER 7

Session Topic
God's holiness has been violated by our sin, but He reconciles us to Himself by the death of Jesus.

Session Goals
1. To contrast human anger with God's anger at sin.
2. To outline the means by which God reconciles us to Himself.
3. To write a personal prayer of thanksgiving to God for His reconciliation.

Materials Needed
√ Bible
√ *What Happens When God Answers Prayer*
√ Chalkboard, chalk
√ News magazines or other magazines for *Launching the Lesson*
√ Copies of Response Sheet 5
√ 3 x 5 cards
√ Pencils

Special Preparation
1. Recall times you have been reconciled either to someone you hurt or to someone who hurt you. What was the cost? How did you feel afterward? How did your relationship with the person change? Draw comparisons with our reconciliation with the Lord through the death of Christ.
2. Consider times when human anger is appropriate: perhaps when someone is killed by a drunk driver, or children are exploited, or a marriage is violated.

49

3. Thank the Lord that Christ died so that God could reconcile you to Himself. Try to keep that spirit of thankfulness as you prepare and lead this session.

LESSON PLAN

Launching the Lesson *(15 minutes)*

For most people, "anger" is a negative word. We associate it with lashing out in an uncontrolled emotional outburst. God's anger at sin is different from fickle and unpredictable human anger. But even on a human level, we can all think of times when anger is appropriate. Introduce that idea by beginning the session with this question: **When is anger bad and when is it good?** Let group members discuss the question as you make notes of their responses on the chalkboard, but do not pass judgment on any responses.

Make the transition from human anger to the anger of God. Use news magazines or other magazines to get your group thinking about what might anger God. Divide members into subgroups and give at least one magazine to each subgroup. Ask: **What do you find in these magazines that God would have the right to be angry about?** Look for actions, attitudes, and values which would offend His holiness, His purity, His righteousness.

When subgroups have had some time to search and discuss the magazines, ask for a few examples. Ask members to explain why they think God would be angry at those things.

Make the connection with the text by saying: **Christenson quotes several Scripture passages which speak of God's wrath. The passages say that God is angry when His holiness is violated by our human sinning. That's not appealing to most of us; we like to think of God as loving rather than angry. What are some differences between the anger of God and our human anger?**

Why does God have the right to be angry with sin?

Discovering God's Principles *(25 minutes)*

Chapter 7 tells us that God in His holiness is angry with two classes of sin. We might call these two classes of sin "before" and "after"—that is, before and after accepting Christ as Savior. God is not angry because He hates sinners. He is angry at their sin, their attitudes or actions that offend His righteousness and holiness.

Say, **If God's wrath were the end of the story, our situation would be hopeless. No matter how much we prayed or did good works, we could never be reconciled to God and get out from under His anger. The amazing truth is what God has done to reconcile us to Himself from our original state of sin, and to keep reconciling us when as believers we fail and commit sin.**

Distribute copies of Response Sheet 5. Ask several people to read Romans 5:1-11 aloud. Direct members to fill in the answers they find in the Scriptures as you work together in a large group to discuss the passage. Use these questions to help members grasp the greatness of what God has done for us in Christ:

- How is our state of being reconciled to God the opposite of being under His wrath?
- How does God make reconciliation possible?
- What are the similarities between the reconciliation of a person in the natural state of sin, and the reconciliation of a Christian who has committed sin?
- What doors have been opened by Christ which were previously shut to us?
- How does our reconciliation with God affect our outlook on suffering?
- What is remarkable about Christ's willingness to die for us?
- What hope do we have for the future because we are reconciled to God?

Note: At Evelyn Christenson's prayer seminars, there are usually a significant number of people who pray to receive Christ or make sure of their relationship with Him. Though most members of your group are probably on the "After" side of salvation, be aware that some may still be on the "Before" side. The prayer your members are about to write can be used as a prayer making sure of salvation.

Visual Sketch 2
"Before": God is angry at that state of sin into which we are all born.
"After": God is angry at the sins which believers commit.

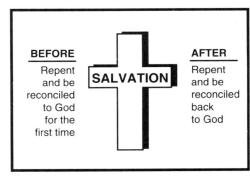

BEFORE
Repent and be reconciled to God for the first time

SALVATION

AFTER
Repent and be reconciled back to God

Applying the Truth (10 minutes)

Ask: **What statement in this passage do you find most meaningful for yourself?** Give time to scan the passage. As members respond with particular verses or phrases, ask: **Why do you choose that one?**

Ask: **As you read this passage on how God reconciles us to Himself, what would you most like to thank Him for?** Let members respond with brief phrases or ideas.

Prayer Time (10 minutes)

Distribute 3 x 5 cards. Instruct: **Look over the passage and your Response Sheet. Then thoughtfully write a prayer to the Lord, thanking Him for reconciling us to Himself. Keep in mind that we have not reconciled Him to ourselves by our good actions; He has reconciled us to Himself by sending Christ to die for us.**

If you think it is appropriate for your group, add: **God never forces us to be reconciled to Him. We still have a choice of whether to accept or reject His offer. As you write your prayer, if you have never accepted God's gift of reconciliation—or if you are not sure—make your prayer one of accepting Christ's death for you and thanking Him for reconciling you to Himself.**

Have a time of silence as members consider and write their prayers. At the end, you may wish to ask if some members want to share their prayers aloud. Close by voicing your own prayer of thanksgiving to the Lord for reconciling each of you to Himself. Invite any who may have fully accepted Christ's reconciliation for the first time to stay with you for a joint prayer of thanksgiving.

ASSIGNMENT

1. Keep your written prayer of thanksgiving where you'll see it often. Pray it frequently this week, adding or changing as you wish.
2. Read chapter 8 of the text.
3. Pray for anyone to whom you feel unreconciled.

Session Eight

WHEN GOD ANSWERS... "BE RECONCILED TO OTHERS"

TEXT, CHAPTER 8

Session Topic
We can be reconciled to others because of the reconciliation Christ has won for us on the cross.

Session Goals
1. To summarize the problems that come when people are not reconciled to each other.
2. To explore the possibilities of being reconciled with others.
3. To commit to doing our part toward reconciliation with someone.

Materials Needed
√ Bible
√ *What Happens When God Answers Prayer*
√ Chalkboard, chalk
√ 3 x 5 cards, pencils

Special Preparation
1. As you prepare for this session, begin to put its truth into practice. Let the truth sink in that Jesus declares all believers already one in Him. Where there is tension between you and another person, take steps to forgive and be reconciled.
2. Be sensitive to the possibility that your group includes people who need to be reconciled to one another. Perhaps the tension is well hidden, or perhaps the rest of the group feels it. If unreconciled tension is there, it will be an undercurrent during this study. Pray that this session will open minds and hearts.

53

LESSON PLAN

Launching the Lesson *(10 minutes)*

Introduce a sense of what it feels like to have strife in relationships. Draw some jagged lines on the chalkboard. Say: **These lines represent broken relationships and unresolved conflicts between people. What are some words and phrases for how it feels when we are not reconciled with someone?** Among the jagged lines, write whatever group members call out.

The results on the chalkboard will not be pretty. Say: **None of us likes to be in the situation of having a broken relationship, but we've all been there at some time. Is there anything that gives us hope that true reconciliation will be possible?** (Members may respond that with God all things are possible, but sometimes the other person does not want to be reconciled.)

Acknowledge the difficulties of reconciliation and refer to the text by saying: **After hearing Evelyn Christenson speak about forgiveness, a woman called her and screamed that she could never forgive her family members. Evelyn wished she could tell her that Jesus had not really said we must forgive, but she couldn't lie. Humanly speaking, in that situation, we would say "It can never work. Reconciliation is impossible." Yet it happened. We don't know how the woman's family responded, but the woman herself found peace. Let's look at how it was possible.**

Discovering God's Principles *(30 minutes)*

Explain that since this woman's reconciliation looked humanly impossible, we can suspect that there was something supernatural going on. Ask someone to read Ephesians 2:11-18. Explain that Paul was referring to the historic conflict between Jews and Gentiles, who regarded each other with suspicion and disdain. Discuss:

- What had happened to enable Paul, a "Hebrew of the Hebrews," to write such a personal letter to a group of Gentiles? (They had all found commonality in Christ.)
- How did Jesus break down the wall of hostility between Gentile and Jew?
- Evelyn Christenson writes that reconciliation has already been accomplished on the cross of Christ. Our responsibility, she says, is to live out in our daily lives what has already been accomplished for us by Jesus. How does that

truth give us hope for reconciliation among ourselves?
- Have you ever been in conflict with someone, and you waited and waited for the person to come to you and be reconciled, but the person did not come? (Discuss.)

Highlight Christenson's point: **On a human level, it really doesn't matter who is angry.** Whether we are angry with someone, or that person is angry with us, or if the feeling is mutual—the answer from God is the same: "Be reconciled!"
- Amplify that idea by having someone read Matthew 18:15. Ask: **When someone sins against us, who has the responsibility to seek reconciliation? How and why?**
- Compare the opposite situation by having someone read Matthew 5:23-24. Ask: **When we have sinned against someone, so that person is holding it against us, who has the responsibility to seek reconciliation? When and how?**

People may now be feeling that reconciliation is a load on their shoulders with few rewards. Remind them that the angry woman who called Evelyn found reconciliation through forgiving. She decided that regardless of her family's past actions or their present attitude toward her, she could forgive them. And she found peace.
- Ask someone to read Ephesians 4:32. Say: **We're told to forgive each other "just as" Christ has forgiven us. On what basis does Christ offer forgiveness?** (See passage.)
- **What happens within us when we forgive?**

Challenge members to look at the possibilities—especially among Christians—when we live in Christ's reconciliation.

Explain that after Jesus had eaten His last supper with His disciples, He promised comfort because they would be with Him in heaven and would have the Holy Spirit with them in this life. Then, before leaving for the Garden of Gethsemane where He would be arrested, He prayed for Himself and for them. It helps to remember the contrast of Luke 22:24 where the disciples had been arguing among themselves about who was greatest.

Ask a group member to read aloud John 17:20-23. Discuss:
- **Here Jesus expands His prayer to include those who will believe in Him through the disciples' message. That includes us! What all does He ask?** (Search the text.)
- **What results will happen in the world because of our oneness?**
- **To what does Jesus compare the oneness of Christians?**

Draw attention to Evelyn Christenson's point that Jesus does not ask us to be reconciled to each other so that we can *become* one, but because we are *already* one in Him. He considers us one body with Himself as Head (Colossians 1:18).

Applying the Truth *(10 minutes)*

Bring Christ's prayer for unity into some practical issues by asking:
- What happens to our witness for Christ when the people in our community see the following things among our local churches: disunity? resentment? competition?
- On the other hand, what happens to our witness when people see the following things among the churches: a friendly spirit? support for each other's work? cooperation in common efforts?
- What happens to our witness for Christ when we remain unreconciled with a person—either someone we have hurt or someone who has hurt us, or both?
- According to what we have seen today, what is our responsibility, regardless of the other person's reaction?

Ask group members to silently think of the name of a person to whom they need to be reconciled. Distribute cards and ask each member to jot down steps they *could* take to be reconciled. After members have made some private notes about what they could do, ask them to circle the steps they *will* take. Urge them not to circle anything casually, but to be truthful with themselves and God.

Prayer Time *(10 minutes)*

Divide into subgroups. Ask group members to pray for each other that any unreconciled relationships will be reconciled. Discourage members from naming names, but invite members to ask each other to "pray especially for me" or some other indication of a particular need of reconciliation.

ASSIGNMENT

1. Encourage members to carry out the steps of reconciliation on which they decided today.
2. Read Chapter 9 of the text.
3. Ask group members to recall a time something was stolen from them, how they felt, and what happened.

Session Nine

WHEN GOD ANSWERS... "MAKE RESTORATION"

TEXT, CHAPTER 9

Session Topic
Reconciliation with others against whom we have sinned often includes making restitution of some kind.

Session Goals
1. To sense the hurt felt by the victims of our sins.
2. To examine a scriptural example of restitution which came from newfound faith in Jesus.
3. To pray that the Lord will show us where we need to make restitution.

Materials Needed
√ Bible
√ *What Happens When God Answers Prayer*
√ Copies of Response Sheet 6
√ Pencils
√ Chalkboard, chalk

Special Preparation
1. To get a picture of the principle of restitution in Old Testament law, read Exodus 22:1-15, Leviticus 6:1-5, Numbers 5:5-8.
2. Zacchaeus was a tax collector. The very phrase is used as a derogatory term in the Gospels. This type of tax collector collected the indirect taxes of Roman customs (as opposed to direct taxes such as land tax and head tax). The office was sold to the highest bidder, who paid in advance to collect the taxes from a district. "The practice of selling the office built into the system disregard for the taxpayer: the highest bid translated

57

into the most inflated assessments and the highest commissions. . . . An occupation which depends for success on suspicion, intrusion, harassment, and force tends not to attract the most pleasant personalities" (Joel B. Green, Scot McKnight, and I. Howard Marshall, eds., *Dictionary of Jesus and the Gospels,* Downers Grove, Ill.: InterVarsity Press, 1992, pp. 805-6).
3. If possible, ask a store owner or manager to tell your group an experience of receiving restitution—that is, someone stole something from the store and returned it or made up for it, whether freely or compelled by the courts. Tell the business person to mention no names and to leave out details which might identify the thief. (Optional for *Launching the Lesson*)

LESSON PLAN

Building the Body (5 minutes)

Ask how many group members have ever had something stolen from them. Ask them how it felt, whether the article was ever returned, and what they thought the thief should have had to do.

Launching the Lesson (10 minutes)

If you have invited a store owner or manager to talk about receiving restitution, introduce the person and ask for the story. Invite group members to ask questions such as: **Would you rather have the thief pay back what was stolen, go to jail, or both? And why?**

Use Response Sheet 6 to lead people to think more broadly about how it feels not only to have something stolen, but to have any wrong done to them. Distribute Response Sheet 6 and explain that this is a private project. Ask members to fill in the left side. Point out that "what I have lost" may include qualities like trust and friendship as well as material things. Encourage members to be specific about "what I wish the person would do." Ask members to keep their Response Sheets handy.

Discovering God's Principles (25 minutes)

Make the connection with the text by pointing out that perhaps the deepest pain of being hurt by others is that they do not see themselves as wrongdoers. Christenson tells of people who call her, devastated at how a spouse or child has abandoned them apparently without a second thought. It is the selfishness of the one sinning that causes the hurt the victim must endure.

Ask: **When someone has done wrong to us, how does restitution help restore the relationship?** (Among other things, restitution is an acknowledgment of the wrong by the one who did it.)

Have someone read Luke 19:1-10. This is a classic case of someone freely making restitution because he has met Christ. Discuss the Scripture using these questions:

- What does the behavior of Zacchaeus tell us about his attitude toward Jesus?
- When Jesus called him down, why do you think Zacchaeus "welcomed Him gladly"?
- What do you think led Zacchaeus to make fourfold restitution for cheating?
- What do you think restitution did for his victims?
- What do you think it did for Zacchaeus?
- What do you think Zacchaeus said when people asked him why he was making restitution?

As Christenson points out, there is no indication that Jesus demanded that Zacchaeus make restitution. But once he came into right relationship with his Lord, all the cheating of his past loomed before him; and his first thought was to make amends to those he had hurt. He had a new compassion for his victims; in place of greed, he discovered the thrill of seeing his victims repaid.

Applying the Truth *(15 minutes)*

So far in this session you have led group members only to think about what it means to be hurt by others and how good it feels when someone makes restitution to you. Now make the transition to the possibility of *your* needing to make restitution.

Remind your group of the words of the great preacher Jonathan Edwards about the duty of making restitution: "I exhort those who are conscious in themselves that they have wronged their neighbor to make restitution. This is a duty the obligation to which is exceedingly plain." Present this question to your group: **Jonathan Edwards thought the obligation of restitution was "exceedingly plain." Why is it not always "exceedingly plain" to us?**

Point out to the group that while we can never make restitution to God for our sin, we can sometimes make up for the damage we have done to another person.

Ask members to take Response Sheet 6 again. Instruct: **At the** top of the right-hand column, write in: "How others must have felt when I have sinned against them." On the long line in the middle, write in: "What others have lost." On the long line toward the bottom, write in: "What others may wish I would do." (It will help to write those three phrases on the chalkboard.)

This exercise will take some time and will demand thoughtful silence. Some members will be considering certain actions for the first time in light of how they may have hurt someone else.

When most members have finished, use these questions to discuss what they have thought about or discovered:

- What is the value of turning the tables and seeing ourselves from the other person's perspective?
- Were there some actions or attitudes that you saw from another person's perspective for the first time?

Encourage group members to consider steps of restitution by directing their attention to any items at the bottom of the right-hand column, "What others may wish I would do." Remind the group that in her work with Prison Fellowship, Christenson finds that restitution is as good for the sinner as for the one sinned against. Restitution gives the sinner a way to make amends and perhaps restore a relationship. Say: **The Lord may or may not be calling you to make restitution by doing the things listed there. We're going to pray for Him to show us whether we should take action to make restitution, and if so, what we should do.**

Prayer Time *(5 minutes)*

First, ask each person to pray silently over his or her Response Sheet. Then move the group into subgroups or pairs and pray for one another. Pray specifically for wisdom about making any necessary restitution and for the courage to do it.

Since some may regard their writing in this section as personal and private, allow any who wish to remain alone for continued private prayer to do so. But mention also that restitution is embarrassing and difficult. Suggest that if they are considering that course of action, they may benefit from the prayer support of another person.

ASSIGNMENT

1. Encourage group members to take action on any restitution they ought to make.
2. Read Chapter 10 of the text.

Session Ten

WHEN GOD ANSWERS... "RESTORE THAT SINNER"

TEXT, CHAPTER 10

Session Topic
We are responsible to restore a repentant sinner to Christian fellowship and useful ministry.

Session Goals
1. To explain the often-neglected ministry of restoration.
2. To explore the steps to restoration, including the responsibilities of the restorer.
3. To consider whether God is calling us to be His instruments of restoration in someone's life.

Materials Needed
√ Bible
√ *What Happens When God Answers Prayer*
√ Chalkboard, chalk

Special Preparation
1. Review the biblical account of David's sin and Nathan's role in his restoration (2 Samuel 11:1–12:25) and David's prayer of repentance (Psalm 51). You reviewed this Scripture for Session 5 on God's requirements, but this time concentrate on Nathan's role. Note Nathan's confrontation of David, his message of forgiveness and warning, and his reminder of God's love (12:25).
2. Read 1 Corinthians 5:1-5 and 2 Corinthians 1:23–2:11, noting similarities between Paul's treatment of the Corinthians and Nathan's treatment of David, and how Paul urges them to treat the sinner among them in the same way.

LESSON PLAN

Launching the Lesson *(10 minutes)*

Restoring a sinner raises many conflicting emotions, particularly in people who have resisted the same temptations the sinner succumbed to. Illustrate the controversy over restoring a sinner by reminding your group of several prominent Christian leaders who have been exposed in sexual and financial sins. Some of these have merely continued in their ministry, others have left the ministry, and still others have submitted themselves to a time of supervised repentance and renewal, then been restored to prominent positions. Turn the discussion away from the sin and toward what happened afterward by asking: **How do you feel about what happened after the sins of these leaders were revealed?**

After a time of discussion, bring the issue closer to home by saying: **None of us knows all the facts necessary to make a final judgment on these famous cases. Yet we all personally know people who have fallen into sin, and it is those people we need to be primarily concerned about. In today's session we will examine our responsibility to those people.**

Discovering God's Principles *(30 minutes)*

Acknowledge that discovering another Christian's sin is always upsetting. When we try to think of what to do, we may feel anger, sorrow, pity, yearning, grief. We may not even want to see the person restored, thinking *Why should he or she get off so easily?*

Explain that God does not leave restoration of a sinner to the whims of our emotions. He has given us biblical steps to follow.

Supply background to the Corinthian passages: Christians in the busy crossroads city of Corinth faced many worldly temptations. Some Corinthian Christians had given in to sexual immorality. They were disgracing the church; Paul called one man's sin the kind that does not occur even among pagans. Others in the church apparently stood in arrogant defense of this sin. Perhaps they were proud that they were broad-minded enough to accept such a person into their congregation. But thanks to Paul's confrontation and the Holy Spirit's work, the Christians at Corinth repented.

Read 2 Corinthians 1:23–2:10. Discuss what Paul wrote about the restoration of the sinner by asking:

- ■ **What had happened within the sinner?** (See passage. Apparently, he had repented.)

- **How had the rest of the church responded?** (They had disciplined him. It is interesting that this worldly church disciplined one of their own so severely. Perhaps they were still embarrassed and angry at their own guilt.)
- **What was Paul afraid would happen?** (See passage.)
- **What attitude did Paul show toward the sinner?** (Help your group find several clues in the text.)
- **How did Paul restore the entire Corinthian church as well as that particular man?** (The passage cites several details. Among them, Paul praised the Corinthians for living up to his confidence in them and for their obedience. He also let them know how much the entire business has grieved him.)

Say: **In Galatians 6:1, Paul gives the work of restoring sinners to "you who are spiritual." We all hope to fit that category. But if we do, we have a responsibility to let God use us to restore believers caught in sin.**

Discuss the ways which Evelyn Christenson believes we can help restore a sinner. Write each on the chalkboard and leave them there for *Applying the Truth:*

By rebuking (necessary if the sinner has not yet repented)

By forgiving (especially difficult if the sin was specifically against us, forgiveness must be sincere)

By what we are (setting an example of faith and holiness)

By praying for the sinner (sincere intercession requires love; different from praying about the sinner—which does not require love)

By praying with the sinner (pouring out your hearts together to the God who is the Heavenly Father of both of you)

By loving without legalism (the person will perceive and reject any lack of love)

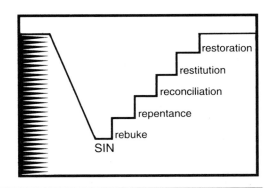

Visual Sketch 3
Steps of Restoration

Say: **The work of restoration is refreshing when we see the sinner returning to God, but it is also draining. Evelyn Christenson reminds us that the true restorer of any sinner is the Lord. He also knows our needs as we do this work, and He can be trusted to restore us, the restorers.**

Continue: **Restoration does not take away all the consequences of sin. After David had committed adultery and murder, God sent Nathan to confront him but also to restore him. To get around David's defenses, Nathan told a brilliant parable about a lamb. David broke down and confessed his sin.**

- Read 2 Samuel 12:13-14. In spite of God's forgiveness, what would be the tragic consequences of the act?
- Read 2 Samuel 12:24-25. How did God send a gracious message through Nathan when Solomon was born?

Applying the Truth *(10 minutes)*

Ask group members to think of a Christian believer who needs the ministry of restoration. Perhaps this person has still not acknowledged his or her sin. Or perhaps there has been repentance but now the person is discouraged and feels like a failure. Ask members to keep that person in mind as you again go over the ways, still on the chalkboard, of restoring a sinner. Have members consider whether they should take any of those steps toward the person. Remind members that the real work of restoring is done by the Lord, but He uses His people to minister His grace to the sinner.

Prayer Time *(10 minutes)*

Ask members to spend a few minutes praying silently for specific Christians who need restoration. Then suggest that they ask God for wisdom in their own actions toward these people. Tell them to ask God what they should do (or refrain from doing) in regard to those people. Then have members pray for each other in their work of restoration. Pray that God will not let you get discouraged and that He will take care of your needs as restorers.

ASSIGNMENT
---

1. Ask members to consider the question: "When is obeying the Lord easiest and when is it most difficult?"
2. Read Chapter 11 of the text.

Session Eleven

WHEN GOD ANSWERS... "NOW OBEY ME"

TEXT, CHAPTER 11

Session Topic
When God answers our prayers, He expects — and rewards — our obedience to what He has told us in His answer.

Session Goals
1. To show that obedience to God requires trust in the Lord.
2. To identify the pain and rewards of Jesus' obedience to the Father.
3. To trust the Lord enough to obey Him in some area where we feel inadequate to obey.

Materials Needed
√ Bible
√ *What Happens When God Answers Prayer*
√ Copies of Response Sheet 7
√ Pencils
√ A clay pot or vase (can be glazed ceramic) for *Launching the Lesson*
√ Words to the first verse of "Have Thine Own Way, Lord"

Special Preparation
1. Consider your own struggles and victories in obeying God — not just in a crisis, but as your ongoing way of life. Think about what you know of God that leads you to trust Him and obey Him.
2. Examine areas of your life where you feel inadequate. (Perhaps one is *leading this study group!*) Thank God that He can and will do through you everything that He calls you to do.
3. Read of Christ's struggles in Gethsemane (Matthew 26:36-46, Mark 14:32-42, Luke 22:39-46). This appears to be the event to which the writer of Hebrews refers in today's passage.

65

| LESSON PLAN |

Launching the Lesson (5 minutes)

Show your group the clay pot you have brought. Use the pot to introduce the idea of being pliable in God's hands by asking:
- **What had to be done to this clay in order to make this?** (It had to be shaped—also decorated and fired, but you are emphasizing the shaping process.)
- **What was the role of the clay?** (to be pliable and yield to the potter)
- **Let's say that this clay has its own personality. What if the clay had refused to be molded into this shape?** (It would have either come out misshapen, or the potter would have set it aside and used another lump of clay.)
- **Why is it vital for the clay to trust the potter?** (The clay does not know the outcome of the potter's work. It must yield to the potter's shaping even if it does not understand the process. If it did not trust the potter, it would resist.)

Explain your illustration by saying: Obeying the Lord is like being a moldable piece of clay in His hands. As we respond to His touch, He makes us into whatever He wants us to be. Our role, as an old hymn says, is to "trust and obey." If we don't trust Him, we'll resist His shaping and we'll miss what He wants to accomplish in us.

Keep the pot on display during the rest of the session.

Discovering God's Principles (30 minutes)

Discuss the following:

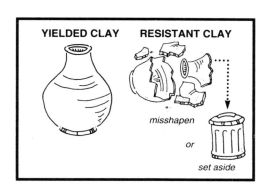

Visual Sketch 4
Yielded Clay vs. Resistant Clay
The role of the clay is to yield and not resist.

- Which do you find is easier—to obey God in the big things or the little things? And why? (Listen to several responses.)
- What have been some of your experiences of trusting the Lord enough to obey Him? What happened as a result?
- Why is trust necessary for obedience?

Explain that Jesus does not ask us to do anything that He has not already done. In the difficult road of obedience, He has gone ahead of us.

Have someone read Hebrews 5:7-10. Point out that the writer was probably referring to Jesus' prayers in Gethsemane, where He finally prayed, "Not My will, but Yours be done" (Luke 22:42). Discuss:

- What do you find in this passage that surprises you? (It is surprising to think that Jesus had to learn obedience or that obedience was difficult for Him. And what does it mean that God "heard" Jesus' prayer to be saved from death—since Jesus chose to die? Resurrection?)
- Why do you think Jesus chose to obey the Father?
- What were the results of Christ's obedience for both Him and us?
- Why was trust necessary for Christ's obedience?
- When we realize that even Jesus struggled to obey His Father—yet He did it—how can that help us?
- If we don't want to obey God at some particular point, what encouragement does this passage offer us?

Use the following activity to remind each other of the good which comes from obeying the Lord. As you do it, you will also encourage each other to keep obeying. Have each group member turn to a neighbor and ask: **What rewards have you found in obeying the Lord?** Give each pair time to ask and answer each other.

Emphasize that in order to obey, we have to trust the Lord. That means not only trusting that God is there, but trusting that He will work good in response to our obedience. The author of the text found that despite her record of obedience, she discovered an area where her faith was lacking. Say: **Evelyn Christenson recounts how, when she was praying in Plymouth, England, God convicted her of the sin of unbelief. She could not understand it. After all, she had traveled all over the world in obedience to the Lord and many times had trusted Him for physical strength and healing. God answered Evelyn, "You do not have enough faith in what I am going to do when you are obedient!"**

Discuss:
- What's the difference between faith in God and faith in faith?
- How does our attitude toward obedience change if we are looking forward to what the Lord is going to do next?

Applying the Truth *(15 minutes)*

Ask: Have you ever looked at what the Lord wanted you to do and said, "Lord, I can't!" (Let members share responses briefly.)

Distribute Response Sheet 7. Instruct: **Think about and identify ways you feel inadequate about obeying God.** What is He asking you to do—or to refrain from doing—which you don't feel able to carry out? Write down why it seems difficult or even impossible for you to obey. Then look up each of the Scripture passages and write down anything that seems to apply to any of your struggles with obedience.

When members have finished writing, invite any who wish to share some of what they have written.

Prayer Time *(10 minutes)*

Divide into small groups of three or four and pray for each other. Pray particularly about areas in which you want to obey the Lord but feel it is difficult. (It is not necessary to give all the details in order to ask for prayer.) As you pray for each other, use your prayers to encourage each other to keep obeying God.

Call attention again to the clay pot. Close your session today by singing together the first verse of "Have Thine Own Way, Lord."

ASSIGNMENT

1. Read Chapter 12 of the text.
2. This week, keep a continuous list of things for which you are thankful to the Lord.

Session Twelve

WHEN GOD ANSWERS...
"HAVE A THANKFUL HEART"

TEXT, CHAPTER 12

Session Topic
If we have a trusting relationship with God, we can include our thanks with our request, thanking Him before He answers.

Session Goals
1. To evaluate the attitudes in which we usually pray.
2. To explore why we can trust God enough to have an attitude of thanksgiving even while we pray.
3. To make a request to God with thanksgiving, thanking Him before He answers.

Materials Needed
√ Bible
√ *What Happens When God Answers Prayer*
√ Copies of Response Sheet 8
√ Pencils

Special Preparation
1. Consider *when* you are most in a spirit of thankfulness to the Lord. Is it right after He has done something for you? When you have a need and are praying? Or some other time?
2. Meditate on the difference between thanking God for what He does and thanking Him for who He is.
3. Read 1 Chronicles 29:1-20, the context of David's prayer. David had wanted to build a permanent temple for the Lord to replace the portable tabernacle. God told David that he was not the one to build the temple, but that his son Solomon would build it — though David would not live to see it.

LESSON PLAN

Building the Body *(5 minutes)*

Ask members to turn first to the person on their right, then to the person on their left, and complete this sentence: "**I have an attitude of gratitude about . . .** "

Share with the whole group what you have an attitude of gratitude about, and why.

Launching the Lesson *(10 minutes)*

Although this chapter of the text concentrates on trusting God enough to thank Him in advance for His answers, that does not cancel out thanking Him *after* He answers. Since the post-answer prayer of thanks is the one with which we are most familiar, set a mood of thankfulness by quoting two Scriptures:

- Colossians 4:2 says "Devote yourselves to prayer, being watchful and thankful." Psalm 118:21 says, "I will give You thanks, for You answered me; You have become my salvation." Why does prayer so often naturally result in thankfulness to God? (Gather several responses.)

Use this illustration and these questions to introduce the idea that it is easier to be thankful after a favor is done than before, but that there might be reasons for being thankful in advance:

- **When we are guests for a meal in someone's home, when do we usually thank them?** (Usually as we are leaving.)
- **Why don't we thank them earlier?** (Discuss.)
- **What value might there be in thanking our hosts as soon as we arrive, before the meal is eaten?** (At that point our thanks is more for the relationship than for the meal. We're thankful for their willingness to share their home with us. Also we are expressing trust that the meal will be good.)
- **When we pray, what value might there be in thanking God in advance for His answers?** (Our thanks at that point would express confidence in God Himself, rather than appreciation for a particular thing He has done for us.)

Discovering God's Principles *(20 minutes)*

Have someone read Philippians 4:6. Discuss:
- **We can all see how it's possible to make prayers and petitions, then *afterward* have thanksgiving. But how is it possi-**

ble to make prayers and petitions *with* thanksgiving? (Giving thanks along with our prayers indicates what we expect.)
- Can you remember a time when you prayed for something and felt thankful *while* you were praying? How do you account for that?

Distribute Response Sheet 8. Make the connection with the text, and lead group members to explore their usual attitudes during prayer, by saying: Evelyn Christenson says that our attitude while making our request to God greatly influences the way we handle His answer. What attitudes do you think Christians often have when we pray? What attitude do you think you typically have when you pray?

Give members time to fill out Response Sheet 8. Then ask:
- What sort of requests do you typically make in an attitude of thanksgiving?
- Why do you think your other requests are usually not made in a spirit of thanksgiving?
- When we fail to have a spirit of thanks when we pray, how might that affect our attitude toward God's answer?
- Evelyn Christenson says it takes deep spiritual maturity to be able to include our thanks with our request. Do you agree? Why might that be true?
- If we are to thank the Lord in advance for His answer to our prayer, what attitude must we have toward Him?

Applying the Truth   *(15 minutes)*

Have group members turn to 1 Chronicles 29:10-13. Explain that David wanted to build a permanent temple for the Lord to replace the tabernacle. The Lord told David that he was not the one to build it, but his son Solomon would build the temple, though David would not live to see it. David assembled all the resources and made all the preparations for building the temple. Then, in front of a huge assembly of people, he praised the Lord in these words. Ask someone to read the passage.

Use this great prayer to talk about the qualities of God which enable us to trust Him. These may seem like simple questions, but they will draw a picture of a great God who can be trusted and thanked in advance for His answers to prayer.
- How long will God last?
- What does God possess?
- What comes from God?

- What can God do?
- Why is God worthy of praise?
- What is God the Lord of?
- What words would you use to describe this God?
- At the end of David's praise, he thanked God. Why was God worthy of being thanked?
- Why would it be safe to thank a God like this in advance for His answers to our prayers?

Say: Evelyn Christenson quotes her daughter Jan as saying that real thankfulness depends on who is in control of your life. As Evelyn explains it, only when we have arrived at an adequate view of God *before* praying can the attitude of thanksgiving be there *while* praying.

Invite people to reconsider their attitudes by looking again at what they wrote on Response Sheet 8. Say: **Let's look especially at the prayers which we find hard to pray with thanksgiving. If we kept in mind the God David prayed to when we pray, what difference would it make in our attitude?** (This God can be trusted to answer in the right way. When we trust Him, we are disposed to be already thankful for His good answer.)

Prayer Time *(10 minutes)*

Turn group members' attention to "My Request" at the bottom of Response Sheet 8. Say: **Take a few minutes to make a special request of the Lord, only make it with thanksgiving. Maybe it's a prayer you've prayed before, but you prayed with a different attitude. This time, thank God for His answer even as you make the request. Write your request unless it is too personal.**

As you pray together, whether in small groups or as a large group, as you choose, thank the Lord for the time you have spent together in this study on what happens when God answers. Ask God to keep you alert to His continuing involvement in everything you have prayed about or will pray about. Ask Him to keep you looking for what He wants to do with His answers, and invite Him to work through you to answer more prayers.

It will be a blessing to your group if they hear you end this final study by praying a prayer of thanks for them and for the privilege of leading this study.